ruach 5765 songbook

includes CD (also available separately)

Editor

Joel N. Eglash

Project Manager & Typesetter

Eric S. Komar

Transcontinental Music Publications
The world's leading publisher of Jewish music since 1938

Visit **www.RuachCD.com**
for artist information, educational material, and downloads

Hebrew Pronunciation Guide

VOWELS
a as in *father*
ai as in *aisle* (= long *i* as in *ice*)
e = short *e* as in *bed*
ei as in *eight* (= long *a* as in *ace*)
i as in *pizza* (= long *e* as in *be*)
o = long *o* as in *go*
u = long *u* as in *lunar*
' = unstressed vowel close to ə or unstressed short *e*

CONSONANTS
ch as in German *Bach* or Scottish *loch* (not as in *cheese)*
g = hard *g* as in **g***et* (not soft *g* as in **g***em*)
tz = as in *boats*
h after a vowel is silent

RUACH 5765 SONGBOOK: NEW JEWISH TUNES ISRAEL

© 2005 Transcontinental Music Publications
CD © 2005 Transcontinental Music Publications
CD: Executive Committee: Hope Chernak, Yonatan Glaser, & Cantor Alane Katzew
Executive Producer : Joel Eglash

A division of the Union for Reform Judaism
633 Third Avenue - New York, NY 10017 - Fax 212.650.4119
212.650.4101 - **www.TranscontinentalMusic.com** - tmp@urj.org

Manufactured in the United States of America
Cover design by Pine Point Productions - Windham, ME
Book design by Joel N. Eglash
ISBN 8074-0958-8
10 9 8 7 6 5 4 3 2 1

PREFACE

RUACH IS THE HEBREW WORD FOR *SPIRIT*. It is exactly *that* quality which the songs of the *Ruach* series possess. What makes *Ruach 5765* different is its theme - songs of or about Israel. We believe that our youth can connect to Israel in a unique way through music. The songs contained herein are reflections of modern Israel, from the perspectives of Israeli and North American musicians. Combining the two into the same collection offers intriguing possibilities. Look deep into the lyrics and music, and you will find exactly what makes Israel the central place that it is in so many of our lives.

The *Ruach* series is the continuation of the seven original NFTY (North American Federation of Temple Youth) albums that were recorded between 1972 and 1989 (see the NFTY five-CD set available from Transcontinental Music). The NFTY and *Ruach* albums are primary sources of participatory music for cantors, songleaders, musical leaders and all those who disseminate Jewish music. Through their leadership, the tradition of singing is passed on to the next generation of campers and youth groupers: the future songleaders, cantors and musical leaders. This songbook is another way of preserving this musical tradition for future generations.

Thanks are due to Lauren Dubin, Michael Goldberg, Jonathan Hall, Scott Hertz, Eric Komar, Victor Ney, Sami Rudnick; to the members of the *Ruach 5765* committee, whose varying backgrounds and experiences helped shape this remarkable collection of music; and of course the artists who have created this great music for all of us.

Joel N. Eglash
Transcontinental Music Publications/Union for Reform Judaism
25 Elul 5765 - 28 September 2005

RUACH 5765 COMMITTEE

Cantor Jill Abramson
Rubin Arquilevich
Hope Chernak
Rabbi Andrew Davids
Joel Eglash
Rabbi Dan Freelander
Jeremy Gimbel
Yonatan Glaser
Cantor Alane Katzew
Rabbi Hara Person

ruach 5765

am yisraeil chai by noam katz

the Jewish people live

> *In Luganda, a native dialect of Uganda, most spoken words end with a vowel sound. The Abayudaya have adopted this speech pattern in their pronunciation of Modern Hebrew. This song reflects that melding of two cultures, the two languages interacting with each other to reveal one universal message – that the strength of God and the Jewish people will live on forever. [Noam Katz]*

Ecstatically (♩= 86)

Am - eh, am - eh, am - eh Yis - ra - eil - eh chai,___

Am - eh, am - eh, am - eh Yis - ra - eil - eh chai.___

Oh,___ oh,___ Od - eh A - vi - nu chai,___

Oh,___ oh,___ Od - eh A - vi - nu chai.___

Repeat from Section A as desired

Note: Originally recorded in the key of F Major (Capo I)

עַם יִשְׂרָאֵל חַי! עוֹד אָבִינוּ חַי! *The Jewish people lives! Our Sovereign yet lives!*

shirat hasticker *by* hadag nachash (snakefish)

the bumper sticker song

words: david grossman, **music:** hadag nachash

ruach
57 ● 65
track 2

> This unusual song, which took Israel by storm to become a chart-topping hit, is based on the words of bumper stickers. They were collected and transformed into poetry by David Grossman, an Israel Prize winning author and leftist social commentator. Far from simply expressing liberal sentiment, the song holds up a mirror to an array of social, cultural, and political issues using the original divisive, ironic, humorous, simplistic, and even shocking words with which Israelis spoke their minds through the stickers. This complex weave of authentic, insider Israeli expressions is produced by HaDag Nachash (Snakefish), one of Israel's leading rock/hip-hop bands. The controversial song, each line of which needs unpacking to be fully understood by someone who has not lived in or followed events in Israel closely, is a window into the kaleidoscopic and intense experience of life in Israel. RuachCD.com contains not only the words translated in English, but also background to the meaning, context, and themes of the song's words. [Yonatan Glaser]

דּוֹר שָׁלֵם דּוֹרֵשׁ שָׁלוֹם.	*A whole generation demands peace.*
תְּנוּ לְצָה"ל לְנַצֵּחַ.	*Let the IDF win.*
עַם חָזָק עוֹשֶׂה שָׁלוֹם.	*A strong people makes peace.*
תְּנוּ לְצָה"ל לְכַסֵּחַ.	*Let the IDF take them down.*
אֵין שָׁלוֹם עִם עֲרָבִים, אַל תִּתְּנוּ לָהֶם רוֹבִים.	*No peace with Arabs; don't give them guns.*
קְרָבִי זֶה הֲכִי, אָחִי.	*There is no service like combat service, bro.*
גִּיּוּס לְכֻלָּם, פְּטוֹר לְכֻלָּם.	*Draft for all or exemption for all.*
אֵין שׁוּם יֵאוּשׁ בָּעוֹלָם.	*There is no despair in the world.*
יֵשָׁ"ע זֶה כָּאן.	*Judea, Samaria and Gaza are here!*
נַ נַח נַחְמָן מֵאֻמָּן.	*Na, Nah, Nahman, the faithful.*
No Fear, מָשִׁיחַ בָּעִיר.	*No Fear, the Messiah's in town.*
אֵין עֲרָבִים אֵין פִּיגוּעִים.	*No Arabs – no terror attacks.*
בַּגָּ"ץ מְסַכֵּן יְהוּדִים.	*The Supreme Court endangers Jews.*
הָעָם עִם הַגּוֹלָן.	*The people are with the Golan.*
הָעָם עִם הַטְּרַנְסְפֶר.	*The people are for [population] transfer.*
טֶסְט בְּיַרְכָּא.	*Test in Yarka [sticker of a vehicle inspection garage in the village of Yarka].*
חָבֵר, אַתָּה חָסֵר.	*Friend, you are missed.*
הַקָּדוֹשׁ בָּרוּךְ הוּא, אֲנַחְנוּ בּוֹחֲרִים בְּךָ.	*The Holy One, blessed be God, we choose You.*
בְּחִירָה יְשִׁירָה זֶה רַע.	*Direct elections [for prime minister] are bad.*
הַקָּדוֹשׁ בָּרוּךְ הוּא, אֲנַחְנוּ קַנָּאִים לָךְ.	*The Holy One, blessed be God, we are Your zealots.*
יָמוּתוּ הַקַּנָּאִים.	*Death to zealots [or "death to the jealous" if the sticker appears on very old cars]*

פזמון	CHORUS
כַּמָּה רַע אֶפְשָׁר לִבְלֹעַ?	*How much evil can you swallow?*
אַבָּא תְּרַחֵם, אַבָּא תְּרַחֵם.	*Father have mercy, Father have mercy.*
קוֹרְאִים לִי נַחְמָן וַאֲנִי מְגַמְגֵּם.	*They call me Nachman and I stutter.*
כַּמָּה רַע אֶפְשָׁר לִבְלֹעַ?	*How much evil can you swallow?*
אַבָּא תְּרַחֵם, אַבָּא תְּרַחֵם.	*Father have mercy, Father have mercy.*
בָּרוּךְ הַשֵּׁם אֲנִי נוֹשֵׁם.	*Thank God I'm breathing.*

מְדִינַת הֲלָכָה – הִלְכָה הַמְדִינָה.	A State based on halachah is no State at all.
מִי שֶׁנּוֹלָד הִרְוִיחַ.	He who is born wins.
יְחִי הַמֶּלֶךְ הַמָּשִׁיחַ.	Long live the Messiah.
יֵשׁ לִי בִּטָּחוֹן בַּשָּׁלוֹם שֶׁל שָׁרוֹן.	I trust the peace of [Ariel] Sharon.
חֶבְרוֹן מֵאָז וּלְתָמִיד.	Hebron – from time immemorial and forever.
וּמִי שֶׁלֹּא נוֹלָד הִפְסִיד.	He who is not born loses.
חֶבְרוֹן עִיר הָאָבוֹת.	Hebron, city of the Fathers.
שָׁלוֹם טְרַנְסְפֶר.	Peace through Transfer.
כָּהֲנָא צָדַק.	[Rabbi Meir] Kahane was right.
CNN מְשַׁקֵּר.	CNN lies.
צָרִיךְ מַנְהִיג חָזָק.	We need a strong leader.
סַתְחִין עַל הַשָּׁלוֹם, תּוֹדָה עַל הַבִּטָּחוֹן.	Peace please, thank you for security.
אֵין לָנוּ יְלָדִים לְמִלְחָמוֹת מְיֻתָּרוֹת.	We have no children for needless wars.
הַשְּׂמֹאל עוֹזֵר לָעֲרָבִים.	The Left helps the Arabs.
בִּיבִּי טוֹב לַיְּהוּדִים.	Bibi is good for the Jews.
פּוֹשְׁעֵי אוֹסְלוֹ לַדִּין.	Oslo criminals [should be brought] to justice.
אֲנַחְנוּ כָּאן, הֵם שָׁם.	Us here, they [the Arabs] there.
אַחִים לֹא מַפְקִירִים.	You do not forsake brothers.
עֲקִירַת יִשּׁוּבִים מְפַלֶּגֶת אֶת הָעָם.	Uprooting the settlements divides the people.
מָוֶת לַבּוֹגְדִים.	Death to traitors.
תְּנוּ לַחַיּוֹת לִחְיוֹת.	Let the animals live.
מָוֶת לָעֲרָכִים.	Death to values.

פזמון	CHORUS
לְחַסֵּל, לַהֲרֹג, לְגָרֵשׁ, לְהַטְעוֹת.	Liquidate, kill, expel, mislead.
לְהַדְבִּיר, לְהַסְגִּיר, עֹנֶשׁ מָוֶת, No Fear	No Fear, subdue, quarantine, death sentence.
לְהַשְׁמִיר, לְהַכְחִיד, לְמַגֵּר, לְבַעֵר.	Lay waste, destroy, rout, eradicate.
הַכֹּל בִּגְלָלְךָ, חָבֵר.	It's all your fault, friend.

my heart is in the east *by e18hteen*

(libi b'mizrach)

words & music: dan nichols, **hebrew:** yehudah halevi

"My heart is in the East (Libi b'Mizrach) and I am at the edge of the west." With these words from the poet Y'hudah HaLevi, Dan Nichols expresses the tension of the Jew who lives in two worlds, the physical world of the Diaspora and the emotional world with ties that bond the Jew to the Land of Israel. This powerful connection to Zion is beautifully expressed by the composer from the perspective of one who has not yet set foot in Eretz Yisrael (the land of Israel). [Cantor Alane Katzew]

has so much____ tied____ to you,____ now.____ It's kind of fun-ny how

I a-dore____ some-one I've nev-er met____ be-fore,____ but,

Ch My heart____ is in____ the east.____ (Li - bi,

li - bi b' - miz - rach.) My heart____ is in____ the east.____

V2 I want to see the dawn of hope in your____ eye,

I want to brush the tears____ from your cheek when you cry. I want to smell the blos-soms

in your hair,____ I want to hear the sound of your songs____ in the air.

I want to taste the hon - ey on your____ lips,

לִבִּי בְּמִזְרָח וְאָנֹכִי בְּסוֹף מַעֲרָב. *My heart is in the East, but I am on the edge of the West.*

11

ekdachim shlufim by aviv geffen

a drawn weapon

Many of us only know Israel's army from what we see on TV or read in the newspaper, but this song takes us behind the scenes to what being a citizen who serves in the army is like for young Israelis. As a young solider returns home for a 24-hour visit, we are invited into his thoughts and feelings. Reuniting briefly with his family and his girlfriend, the soldier demonstrates the sacrifices Israelis make to maintain a people's army. Back home the soldier can acknowledge some of the emotions he needs to keep in check while serving. As he sets out to return to his base, he longs to stay with his girlfriend. Waiting for the bus, the radio reports political events that perhaps mean that "peace is coming" The soldier, however, is skeptical and, more than anything else, simply tired.
[Yonatan Glaser]

lif t'a-d' - a-gah bi-n' - shi-kah.
zov da-var___ ya-feh k'-mo she-at.
dam bi-y' - shi-vah v'-cho-leim

A - val b'-to - cho ek-da-chim___ sh'lu - fim,___ a-na-shim___

_ bo - chim,___ ha-ko-tzim___ por - chim.___

A - val b'-to - cho ek-da-chim___ sh'lu - fim,___ zeh ta-mid___

_ ko - eiv___ k'she-hap'-tza-im___ p'tu - chim.

CODA

_ a - le-ha.___

הוּא חָזַר מֵהַצָּבָא. הוּא נִרְאֶה עָיֵף נוֹרָא,
אֲבָל עוֹד מְעַט הוּא כְּבָר מַגִּיעַ.
שְׁבִיל יָשָׁן בַּשְּׁכוּנָה
הוּא חוֹצֶה לָאֲהוּבָה שֶׁמְּחַכָּה.

He returned from the army. He seemed dreadfully tired, but soon he will arrive. An old lane in the neighborhood, he crosses to his love who waits.

הַשְּׁכֵנִים שֶׁבַּחַלּוֹן צוֹחֲקִים, עוֹבְרִים לְדוֹם.
בְּאַפּוֹ הָרֵיחַ שֶׁל הַבַּיִת.
לְאִמּוֹ שֶׁבַּכְּנִיסָה
הוּא מַחֲלִיף תִּדְאָגָה בִּנְשִׁיקָה.

The neighbors at the window laugh, stand at attention. The cooking smells at home. His mother at the entrance. He replaced her worry with a kiss.

אֲבָל בְּתוֹכוֹ אֶקְדָּחִים שְׁלוּפִים,
אֲנָשִׁים בּוֹכִים, הַקּוֹצִים פּוֹרְחִים.
אֲבָל בְּתוֹכוֹ אֶקְדָּחִים שְׁלוּפִים,
זֶה תָּמִיד כּוֹאֵב כְּשֶׁהַפְּצָעִים פְּתוּחִים.

But inside him are drawn revolvers, crying people, blooming thorns. But inside himself he is a drawn weapon, it always hurts when the wounds are open.

13

בַּחַלּוֹן כּוֹכָב עוֹלֶה. הִיא רוֹאָה אוֹתוֹ בּוֹכֶה.
וְאוֹמֶרֶת "גַּם אֲנִי פוֹחֶדֶת."
הוּא עוֹנֶה לָהּ "זֶה קָשֶׁה
לַעֲזֹב דָּבָר יָפֶה כְּמוֹ שֶׁאַתְּ."

At the window a star rises. She sees him cry and says, "I too am afraid." He answers her, "It's hard to leave something as beautiful as you."

וּבָרַדְיוֹ יֵשׁ שִׂיחָה:
דְּמוּת בְּכִירָה בַּמֶּמְשָׁלָה
מַרְגִּישָׁה שֶׁהַשָּׁלוֹם מַגִּיעַ.
הוּא יוֹשֵׁב בַּתַּחֲנָה,
הוּא נִרְדָּם בִּישִׁיבָה וְחוֹלֵם עָלֶיהָ.

And on the radio there is an interview: A senior figure in the government feels that peace is on the way. He sits at the bus terminal, he falls asleep sitting, and dreams of her.

hodu ladonai by stacy beyer

give thanks to God

hebrew: psalm 118:1-4

ruach track 5 57 65

Knowing God's love is everywhere and unending inspires me. I knew that the music for this prayer was going to be very intense, so we decided to use a stringed instrument called a bouzouki for the introduction. It sets up the hard driving tempo that pushes the music and lyrics through to the very end of the song. Let all who praise God say Ki l'olam chasdo … I love the power of that! The thought of us all joining together to feel the boundlessness of God's love is amazing to me. And, at the same time, we can also look within to find that same unending energy, spirit, love and hope. Those gifts that are also forever and everlasting. [Stacy Beyer]

God is good,___ ki____ tov. Ki l'-o-lam___ chas-do,

God's love is nev - er - end - ing, nev - er - end - ing.

It reach - es far - ther than the bound - 'ries___ that you___ and I___ know.

It's ev - ery-thing___ we are___ and ev - ery-where___ we___ go.___ Let the

house of Is - rael say,___ let the house of Aa - ron say,___ let all___

_ who praise___ God say,___ ki l' - o - lam chas - do.___ Let the

house of Is - rael say,___ let the house of Aa - ron say,___ let all___

_ who praise___ God say,___ ki l' - o - lam, ki l' - o - lam___ chas -

do.

הוֹדוּ לַיְיָ כִּי טוֹב. כִּי לְעוֹלָם חַסְדּוֹ. *Give thanks to God, for God is good. For God's love is everlasting.*

the hope by rick recht

hebrew: n. h. imber

For 2000 years, Jews yearned to be a free people in the land of Zion and Jerusalem. Rick Recht's original lyrics express this hope, which became a reality with the founding of M'dinat Yisraeil, the State of Israel, in 1948. Israel is central to the emergence of our Jewish identity; it serves as the glue "that holds us together." [Cantor Alane Katzew]

broken world by yom hadash

words & music: josh nelson

> In Israel, the Middle East, and the world over, religious consciousness is all too often a source of conflict, but it can just as easily be a source of healing. The title "Broken World" reflects the belief of the 16th century Lurianic Kabbalists, who lived in Eretz Yisrael (the Land of Israel), that each moment in life is an opportunity to engage in the work of tikkun olam, the repair of the world. When people see religious and racial diversity as a problem instead of something to celebrate, we can find hope in two ideas: that we all inhabit and are part of the same created world, and that we can all experience the world as broken and in need of repair. As we hope and work for better times in Israel, awareness of these facts can give us strength and hope for ourselves and humanity. [Cantor Alane Katzew, Yonatan Glaser]

Passionately (♩ = 90)

Can__ you ex-plain__ this? Give__ me an an - swer.

These ques-tions__ are haun-ting__ me.__ Stare a-cross__ these bor - ders.

How are we__ so dif - ferent? The same col - or____ when we__ bleed.__ For__ time

has brought us__ life, brought__ us love, brought__ us face__

_ to face,__ but We breathe the__ same air, see the__ same

sky,   but you and___ I___ live in a bro-ken___ world.___   I see my___ dreams___

___ with-in your___ eyes,___   but you and___ I___ live in a bro-ken___ world.___

These cuts___ run deep - er   than dark - ened wa - ters.

They draw an___ in - vis - i - ble___ line.___   For all___ this an - ger

and cold___ frus-tra - tion,   is your peace___ the same as___ mine?___ For___ time___

(Instrumental)

V3

Em⁷ ... **Cadd⁹** ... **G**

May___ your chil - dren   and may___ my chil - dren   nev-er know_____ this

D   **Cadd⁹** ... **Em⁷**

world   we___ see.____   Our time___ is pass - ing

Cadd⁹ ... **G** ... **D**   **Cadd⁹**   *D.S. %% al Coda*

in fleet - ing mo - ments   like a mir - ror___ of mem-o - ries.___ For___ time___

CODA

G ... **Am⁷** ... **G/B**

We breathe the___ same   air,   see the___ same   sky,   but you and___ I___

C ... **D** ... **G**

___ live in a bro - ken___ world._____   I   see   my___ dreams___

Am⁷ ... **G/B** ... **C**   **D**

___ with - in   your___ eyes,____   but you and___ I____ live in a bro - ken

G ... **Am⁷** ... **G/B** ... **C**   **D**

world.

G ... **Am⁷** ... **G/B** ... **C**   **D**   *Repeat (ad lib.)*
and fade

fanan by the fools of prophecy (shotei han'vuah)

cool

text: gilad vital, **music:** gilad vital & amit carmeli

> A seemingly simple song about a boastful but confused young man, a deeper look at the words with their myriad Jewish and Israeli references shows us someone in the throes of an identity crisis. Feeling at the same time strong and weak, hopeful and despairing, connected and alienated, this young man reflects many of the tensions in Israeli identity and life. Nostalgic for past times yet realizing that we can not turn the clock back, the song references the Torah and the Prophets, the destruction of the Temple, Zionist mythology and heroes, an American TV show of the '70s, the Israeli army, a contemporary Israeli song, and the daily news. Drawing on multiple ethnic music sources, the band's very name—Fools of Prophecy—tells us that they know that the line between truth telling (like prophets) and self-delusion (like people who think they are prophets) is a fine one. With smart, thoughtful musicians like these, we just might be able to tell the difference. And what a musical ride while we are working on it [Yonatan Glaser]

שׁוּב אֲנִי הוֹלֵךְ בְּמַחֲשָׁבוֹת מִתְהַפֵּךְ,
מְגַלְגֵּל אֶת הָעֵינַיִם, וְיוֹשֵׁב לְיָד הַמַּיִם,
כֵּן הוּא אִתִּי עַכְשָׁיו בְּכָל מָקוֹם, בְּכָל מַצָּב
בְּאֶרֶץ שֶׁל הַדְּבַשׁ זָבַת הֶחָלָב.
תַּגִּידִי לִי מִי בָּא בַּתּוֹר, מִי בָּא לְקָרֵב
וְאַל יִתְהַלֵּל חוֹגֵר עַל שְׁכֵנָיו.
הַאִם יָגוּר זְאֵב עִם כֶּבֶשׂ אִם נִפְגַּע בַּמַּטָּרָה?
הַתֹּכֶן שׁוּב מֵעִיד כֵּן שׁוּב מֵעִיד עַל הָעִסָּה.

Again I walk with tumbling thoughts
Roll the eyes and sit near the water
Yes, he is with me now at every place, in every situation, in the land of the milk and honey.
Tell me who comes in line, who comes to bring closer
And don't praise the one who binds his neighbor
Will the wolf dwell with the lamb if we hit the target?
The content bears witness, yes again, witnesses the dough.

הַכֹּל יִהְיֶה בְּסֵדֶר. הַכֹּל יִהְיֶה פָנָאן.

Everything will be fine, everything will be cool

כֵּן, אֲנִי רָבְתִּי עִם סְטִיב אוֹסְטִין
וְנִצַּחְתִּי בְּשַׁחְמָט אֲנִי כַּזֶּה גָּדוֹל,
אֲנִי אַף פַּעַם לֹא אֶפֹּל.
הַדּוֹד שֶׁלִּי זֶה מֹשֶׁה, אֲנִי אוֹכֵל עַד שֶׁנֶּחְנָק.
אֲנִי גָּדוֹל וְיֵשׁ לִי חֲבֵרִים בַּשָּׁבַּ"כ.
מָתַה לָנוּ כָּל הַפְּאוֹרָה לַחֲלוֹם הַזֶּה
לִהְיוֹת, לִרְקֹד כָּאן הוֹרָה.
קַר, מְנֻכָּר, מְסֻנְוָר
מֵהַבְּזָקֵי הַטֶּכְנוֹלוֹגְיָה וְהַשִּׁיר שֶׁלֹּא נִגְמָר.
שִׁירוּ שִׁיר לַשָּׁלוֹם כִּי עוֹד לֹא מְאֻחָר,
הָרוּחַ וְהַמַּיִם עֲדַיִן אוֹמְרִים אוֹתוֹ דָּבָר
וְזֶה קוֹרֶה בְּדִיּוּק עַכְשָׁיו פֹּה.
הַקֶּרַח פֹּה נִשְׁבָּר.

Yes I argued with Steve Austin
And I won at chess I am so great,
I will never fall.
My uncle is Moshe, I eat till I choke.
I am fabulous and I have friends in the secret service.
All the splendor has expired for this dream to be,
to dance the Hora here.
Cold, alienated, blinded from the flashes of technology
and the song that never ends.
Sing a song of peace because it is never too late.
The wind and the water still say the same thing
and it happens right now here.
The ice breaks up here.

הַכֹּל יִהְיֶה בְּסֵדֶר. הַכֹּל יִהְיֶה פָנָאן.

Everything will be fine, everything will be cool

working for shalom by beth schafer

When America went to war in Iraq, many people fell on both sides of the fence on whether we should be there. What struck me most, however, was the massive amount of intelligence and raw talent that was being used to add to the destruction of the world and human spirit. When the most graceful people are the fighters, and not the dancers, when the most intelligent leaders are marching to war and not standing for peace, and when we talk more than we listen, something has got to change. Working for Shalom is a commitment to use my energy, my talent and my influence to always take steps toward peace. May we all be humble enough to know that the preservation of humankind is more important than the preservation of our individual pride. May each person, when they recognize what their God-given talent is, find a way to use it to make peace in the world. [Beth Schafer]

NB: All D and B chords can be played as Dadd⁹ and Badd⁹, respectively.

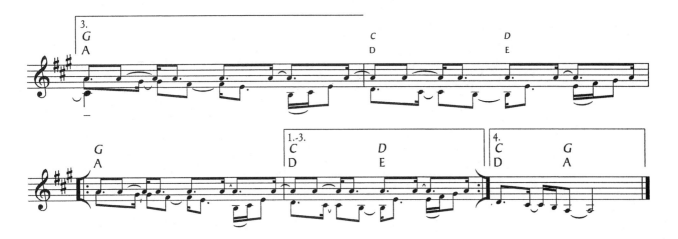

war no more by steve dropkin

words: isaiah 2:4

Reflecting the composer's frustration with the ongoing struggle for peace in the Middle East, the contemporary loud-soft dynamics of this setting evoke the hopeful yet realistic tone of Isaiah's words. Steve Dropkin purposefully uses the seemingly meaningless word na, which is actually an idiomatic Hebrew expression for "please." To represent his personal anger, he puts the stress into the heavier sections of the song, on the repeated Hebrew phrase Lo yisa goi el goi cherev, lo yilm'du od milchamah (Nation shall not lift up sword against nation, and they shall study war no more), while the more mantra-like verse is in the translated English. Though the chord underneath his ending phrase, war no more, is dark, his message remains optimistic. [Joel Eglash]

Na-tion shall not___ lift up sword a-gainst na - tion,___

and they shall stud - y___ war no___ more.___

_ Na-tion shall not___ lift up sword a-gainst na - tion,___ and they shall stud - y

war no___ more, war no___ more. War no___ more.___

1.
War no___ more.___

2.
War no___ more.___

Lo yi - sa goi___ el goi che-rev,___ lo yil - m'-du___ od

mil - cha - mah.___ Lo yi - sa goi___ el goi che-rev,___

lo yil - m'-du___ od mil - cha - mah.___

War no___ more.

לֹא יִשָּׂא גוֹי אֶל גּוֹי חֶרֶב,
לֹא יִלְמְדוּ עוֹד מִלְחָמָה.

Nation shall not lift up sword against nation,
nor ever again shall they train for war.

or chadash by neal katz

a new light

text & music: neal katz & alan cook, based on *yotzeir or*

> The new Reform prayer book, Mishkan T'filah, reinstates this prayer for messianic redemption, full of meaning for religious Zionists, to its original place at the conclusion of the Yotzeir in Shacharit (morning service) after an absence of 150 years. Changing perceptions and the birth of the State of Israel in 1948 saw the rise of a Reform Zionist voice in North America and assured the eventual return of Or Chadash, the petition to "shine a new light upon Zion, that we all might merit its radiance."

Or cha - dash, a new light will shine. Al Tzi - yon ta - ir,__ on Je-ru - sa-lem. Bring-ing us home to the land of our peo-ple. Or cha - dash, and a new light will shine.___

Un - to Av - ram You is-sued a com - mand. Lech l'-cha,__ and I'll show you a new land. And a cov - e-nant__ was sworn that our na - tion would__ be born, and we'd grow to be__ num-'rous as the sand. Or cha-

Driv-en a - way for hun-dreds of years.__ In a

אוֹר חָדָשׁ עַל צִיּוֹן תָּאִיר. לֵדְּ-לְדָּ.   *A new light will shine upon Zion. Go forth.*

ba baahavah by sheva

come in love

text & music: Amir Paiss

> Ba BaAhavah *was initially written as a letter to a desperate friend, as a way to share with him some of Life's useful keys, collected during years of travel and study. The song is a kind of a key holder... reminding us of our immediate connection with our source, with Love, with Truth. Reminding us to remember that we are all members of God's creation, that God's language is Love, that our seemingly separate existence is an illusion and that we are in fact so interconnected, and therefore responsible for what is happening in the world we share. Borders and boundaries have been well manipulated by those forces that want to use fear as a controled measure. We refuse to be paralyzed by fear, we know that reality is genuinely ruled by love, and Love is what we choose to live by and manifest through all of our relations during our lifetime.*
>
> *It is not in the hands of anyone else but ours, we change the world through the healing powers of Love.*
> *It is as simple as breath.*
>
> [Amir Paiss of Sheva]

33

Dai dai dai dai dai dai dai dai dai dai dai. Dai dai dai dai dai dai

dai dai dai dai dai dai.____ Dai dai dai dai dai dai dai dai dai dai dai.____

A - na al ti - ka - na____

v'-al____ ti - ma - na l' - hak-shiv_____ el ha-leiv.____

אָנָא אַל תִּכָּנַע וְאַל תִּמָּנַע לְהַקְשִׁיב אֶל הַלֵּב.
תִּתְאַזֵּן, תִּשְׁתַּלֵּב וְתַקְשִׁיב, תַּקְשִׁיב לֵב.
תִּתְיַצֵּב בְּאָדָם בְּאָדָם וְהַ"מַּה" יֵהָפֵךְ לַ"זֶה".
הַמַּרְאוֹת מִסְּבִיבְךָ רַק מוֹרוֹת לְךָ - אַל דְּאָגָה.
הַגֹּלֶם גֹּלֶם וְהַפָּר פָּר.

Please don't give up and don't avoid listening to your heart.
Balance, interweave and listen, listen to your heart.
Stabilize the humanity in your humanness and the "what" will turn to "it".
The mirroring sights around you only show you no worries.
The dummy is the cocoon and then the butterfly.

תִּתְנַזֵּר, תִּשְׁתַּפֵּר, תְּמַחְזֵר,
תַּחֲזֹר אַחֲרֵי חַיִּים וּבָהֶם תִּתְאַהֵב.
תְּצַפֶּה – תִּתְאַכְזֵב, תִּתְעוֹרֵר, תִּצְטַעֵר,
וְתִכְאַב, וְתֶאֱהַב וְתִרְאֶה הַנִּרְאֶה שֶׁבַּכֹּל.
וְתַוַּתֵּר, כֵּן, תְּוַתֵּר עַל הַצֹּרֶךְ וּמָה הָאֹרֶךְ שֶׁל זֶה,
אִם לֹא זֶה הַמַּחֲזֶה שֶׁאַתָּה רוֹצֶה לְהִכָּתֵב.

Abstain, improve, recycle, woo life and fall in love with it.
Expect and you'll get disappointed, wake up, feel sorry and ache and love and see what is seen in everything.
And let go, yes let go of the need and of what is the length of it, if this is not the play you want to be written.

הַבָּא בְּאַהֲבָה, בָּא בְּאַהֲבָה בָּא
בְּאַהֲבָה בָּא בְּאַהֲבָה בָּא בָּאָה
הַבָּא בָּאָבָּא אָהָה וּבָא בְּאַהֲבָה.

The one who comes in love,
comes in love, comes in love...

תִּתְפַּשֵּׁט מִקְּלִיפוֹת הֶעָבָר שֶׁנִּגְמַר וָמֵת
וְתִהְיֶה הַנּוֹלָד שֶׁבָּא כָּאן וְאַכְשָׁיו.

Strip the shells of the past that have passed and died and be the newly born. That comes in the here and now.

'Cause God is life and life is love;
'Cause life is God and God is love.

'Cause God is life and life is love;
'Cause life is God and God is love.

מַסֵּכָה זֶה פָאסֶה.

Masks are passé. Do you think so? Your love is your beauty, is trust in oneself, and your duty to be. Evolution is now.

Do you think so? Your love is your beauty, is trust in oneself, and your duty to be. Evolution is now.

זֶה עָמוֹק, זֶה שָׁטְכִי, זֶה הַצְּחוֹק, זֶה הַבְּכִי
שֶׁל כָּל הַכַּדּוּר וְהַסֵּדֶר בָּרוּר
כְּשֶׁיֵּשׁ סֵדֶר בְּךָ
זֶה הַשָּׁלוֹם מִשְׁפָּחָה בָּא בְּךָ.

It is profound, it is superficial. It is the laughing, it is the crying of the whole ball and the order is clear when there is order in you. There is peace amongst the family. It comes, it comes in you

אַל תְּאַחֵר לְהִתְעוֹרֵר, אַל תִּסְתַּגֵּר,
אַל תְּשַׁקֵּר, אַל תְּמַהֵר. הַחִפָּזוֹן מִין הַשָּׂטָן הוּא,
מִין תַּחֲרוּתִי, מִין הָאַשְׁלָיָה.
וְאַתָּה לֹא צָרִיךְ שׁוּם מְתַוֵּךְ בֶּנְךָ לְבֵין הָאֱלֹהִים
לְהֱוָיָה, לַחֲוָיָה.

Don't be late to wake, don't close yourself in, don't lie, don't hurry. Haste is a type of devil, a type of competition, a type of illusion. And you need no mediator between yourself and God and Being and Experiencing

אָז תִּתְקַשֵּׁר, תְּאַשֵּׁר וְתִהְיֶה מְאֻשָּׁר.
תְּנַתֵּב עַצְמְךָ בָּרִקּוּד, זֶה מֻתָּר.
הָאֱמֶת הִיא פְּשׁוּטָה כְּמוֹ הַנְּשִׁימָה.

So communicate, acknowledge and you will be acknowledged. Navigate yourself in the dance, all is allowed. Truth is as simple as breathing.

אָנָא אַל תִּכָּנַע וְאַל תִּמָּנַע לְהַקְשִׁיב אֶל הַלֵּב.

Please don't give up and don't avoid listening to your heart.

[Translation: Yonatan Glaser]

hatikvah
the hope

text: N.H. Imber, **music:** based on a Czech folk song

> Israel's national anthem in new musical clothes by a band known for being witty and biting, this song is a delightful fusion of Israeli Mizrachi pop, Eastern and Western rock and hip-hop, and traditional influences from all over. The band's name, which they transliterate in their tongue-in-cheek style into the English "Tea packs," is actually the name for correction fluid in Hebrew. That is a reference to the band members' origins in a poor town, known in Israel as a development town, where they felt, growing up, "whited out" or invisible. Now a much-loved band with many hit records, recording the national anthem is an unexpected choice for a band whose lyrics normally take an ironic view of the trials and tribulations of daily life. That they did so perhaps indicates the deep connection many Israelis have with their country not only as the place where they live, but also as the homeland of their own, deep Jewish identification, a place where historic longing, the aspiration of national independence, and the Jewish spirit come together as one in the name of the One. [Yonatan Glaser]

Solemnly (♩ = 72)

capo 3: Am / Cm ... Dm / Fm ... Am / Cm

Kol___ od ba-lei-vav p'ni - - mah
(p' - ni - mah)

Dm / Fm ... Am / Cm ... E7 / G7 ... Am / Cm

ne - fesh Y'-hu - di ho - mi - yah ul'-fa-a-tei___ miz - rach

כָּל עוֹד בַּלֵּבָב פְּנִימָה
נֶפֶשׁ יְהוּדִי הוֹמִיָּה
וּלְפַאֲתֵי מִזְרָח קָדִימָה
עַיִן לְצִיּוֹן צוֹפִיָּה

עוֹד לֹא אָבְדָה תִקְוָתֵנוּ
הַתִּקְוָה (בַּת) שְׁנוֹת אַלְפַּיִם
לִהְיוֹת עַם חָפְשִׁי בְּאַרְצֵנוּ
אֶרֶץ צִיּוֹן וִירוּשָׁלַיִם.

So long as still within the inmost heart a Jewish spirit sings, so long as the eye looks eastward, gazing toward Zion,

our hope is not lost – the hope of two thousand years: to be a free people in our land, the land of Zion and Jerusalem.

artist biographies

STACY BEYER graduated college at the age of 19 (began at the age of 13), with a Major in Music. She has toured the world as a secular artist and has written music for television and films. When she moved to Nashville in 1990, she was a recording artist and wrote for EMI Music Publishing for 5 years, starting in 1995. She's had songs recorded by Tracy Byrd, Steve Azar, and many others. As Jewish music began to emerge as the musical center of her life, Stacy recorded two original Chanukah songs for a Warner Brothers Records project entitled *A Children's Chanukah*. Recently, Stacy released a new Chanukah recording featuring these and other original Chanukah songs for a project that has been commissioned by her own congregation. As an Artist in Residence at Temple Ohabai Sholom in Nashville, Stacy is a Cantorial Soloist and Jr. Choir Director. She has performed regionally for 14 years for B'nai B'rith, Hadassah, NCJW, Youth Camps, JCC, Jewish Federation, URJ Regional Biennials, and much more. Stacy has performed at CAJE and her song *Find Your Voice* was the theme of the opening and closing concerts at CAJE 29. Her music is quickly finding its way into services, religious schools and more. With the release of her 2nd CD, Stacy has launched her first national tour as a Jewish Contemporary Recording Artist. Her Ha Makom - The Place Tour is giving those that have only heard her recordings an opportunity to experience the raw energy and excitement, as well as the spirited and soulful moments that make Stacy's live performances so memorable. Whether in concert, services or leading songwriting and choir workshops, Stacy's musicianship and dynamic vocal talent continues to capture the attention of her audiences as an emerging force in contemporary Jewish Music.

For over 30 years, **STEVE DROPKIN** has been involved in Jewish music, first songleading at the Eisner Camp in Great Barrington, MA at the age of 14. In high school he was the Regional Songleader for the Jersey Federation of Temple Youth, a region of NFTY. That experience led to his inclusion on three of the NFTY recordings. At college, while majoring in theatre at Clark University in Worcester, MA, Steve's songleading career blossomed. He became widely known for his unique ability to motivate groups in singing and in prayer. He has now led hundreds of retreat weekends and conclaves. Steve has been a regular guest lecturer at the Hebrew Union College-Jewish Institute of Religion School of Sacred Music in New York for over 10 years. His presentations on contemporary Jewish music have been heard by scores of cantorial students who have used his concepts to balance contemporary music with the more traditional Jewish modes. He has also been a guest panelist at the American Conference of Cantors national convention. Even though Steve has been writing songs for little more than 12 years, his songs have found their way into the mainstream of Reform Jewish music. Many of his songs are already "standards" in Reform camps and religious schools, as well as in worship services. He is widely regarded as a major new composer of contemporary Jewish music and liturgy. His powerful song, *If Not Now, When?* was chosen as the New Jersey State Anthem for the first World AIDS Day commemoration. He has been a finalist in the American Jewish Song Festival, as well as the Zionist Organization of America Song Contest. Transcontinental Music has included more than 20 of Steve's songs in numerous projects. You can find his work in *The Complete Shireinu, Shabbat Anthology*, and in *The Complete Jewish Songbook for Children, Volume 2: Manginot*. His songs can also be found on the *Ruach* CDs, as well as a new collection of music called *The Nigun Anthology*. Two of Steve's major pieces have been released in choral settings for synagogue choir. Steve has performed all over the United States, in England, and in Israel. Steve has released his 5th CD entitled *On That Day*, fresh on the heels of his other solo CDs *Innerpeace* and *Keep Our Hopes Alive*. Dropkin's two other CDs were recorded with his former trio, Ketzev. He has two beautiful daughters, Marni and Ariel.

THE FOOLS OF PROPHECY are six human beings, friends by flesh and soul, assembled together in the Holy Land, with a mutual will and quest. Their quest is to enlighten themselves along with their neighbors in Israel and around the globe by experiencing the power and magic of true connection between people. On the musical level, the Fools are playing a fusion of reggae dub, side by side with hip hop and dance – all spiced with an eastern Mediterranean flavor. Doing so the Fools have created their own Israeli style. In the year 2000, the Fools were signed by Helicon Records and released their debut album which reached platinum. The same year they won the prestigious Israeli academy award - BAND OF THE YEAR. The Fools are considered a unique phenomenon in the Israeli music scene, due to their sweeping influence over a vast variety of crowds from different ages and origins. Through their music the Fools unite religious and secular, east and west, Jews, Christians and Muslims.

RABBI NEAL KATZ is an active artist on the Jewish Music scene. Originally from Virginia Beach, VA, Neal has been involved with Jewish music for over fourteen years. He grew up in the youth groups and summer camps of the Reform Movement and has songled for three summers in Israel working with teen Israel trips. Neal has led music for numerous youth group conclaves and congregational services, b'nai mitzvah, Sunday School programs, and retreats around the East Coast and Midwest. In addition to three summers as the student rabbi and songleader at Camp Ben Frankel in Carbondale, IL, Neal songled for a Progressive Jewish Summer camp in the Former Soviet Union. He has a passion for Jewish music and getting people singing. Currently, he is rabbi of Congregation Beth El in Tyler, TX. With his wife, Jennifer Katz, they have a son, Micah, and a daughter, Lila.

NOAM KATZ is one of the newest and most exciting voices in Jewish music today. His soulful melodies, high-flying energy, and sense of humor have delighted audiences throughout North America, Israel and Uganda. A native of Rochester, NY, Noam spent most of his childhood summers at URJ Eisner Camp in Great Barrington, MA. There he immersed himself in a world of Jewish music, learning, and social activism. After spending years as a head songleader at the URJ Kutz and Eisner Camps, Noam was inspired to go on the road during the summer of 2003, bringing his enthusiasm, humor and innovative programs to hundreds of campers and staff at Union for Reform Judaism summer camps. He performed at the 2003 NFTY Convention in Washington, D.C., as well as for over 5000 Reform Jewish leaders at their 2003 Biennial Convention in Minneapolis, MN. Today, Noam continues to share his music and love for Jewish learning with teens, adults and children, touring at camps and congregations of every denomination. In 2001, Noam released his debut album, *Rakia*, a collection of 12 original songs in Hebrew and English. It includes Noam's new melodies for *Modim, Layehudim,* and *Nachshon*. One of the songs, *Halleli*, was selected to be on the 2003 *Ruach 5763* album, a compilation of new Jewish tunes put out by Transcontinental Music. Noam has also served as the cantorial soloist for Temple Isaiah in Lexington, MA. At present, Noam is in the rabbinic program at Hebrew Union College in Jerusalem and working on a sophomore recording with producer Josh Nelson. In the winter of 2003-04, Noam had the extraordinary opportunity to spend three months volunteering with the Abayudaya Jews of Uganda. In addition to teaching Hebrew, English, and Judaics in their schools, Noam organized a youth group, assisted with communal development, and coordinated a cultural show of traditional Abayudaya dance and music. This immersion into a community rich with tradition and an authentic African Jewish identity has greatly influenced Noam's songwriting and has furthered his commitment to teaching social justice and tolerance through his music. In addition to his solo work, Noam has recorded and performed with Peri Smilow and the Freedom Music Project, a gospel choir of young Jewish and African-American singers from the Boston area. In any setting, Noam remains committed to creating strong Jewish and interfaith communities through the unifying power of music.

JOSH NELSON is considered one of the preeminent performers and producers in modern Jewish music. A multi-instrumentalist and songwriter, Josh's music has been celebrated and integrated into the musical consciousness of congregations, camps and communities across the United States. As a founding member of YOM HADASH, Josh has grasped the opportunity to reach multiple generations of American Jews, inspiring and energizing listeners with his unique guitar and piano styles and powerful voice. A wide variety of musical influences appear in his music, ranging from the Beatles, Led Zeppelin, and Motown to Ben Folds, Stevie Wonder, and Miles Davis. Originally a classically trained musician, Josh continues to pursue a Doctoral degree in music while teaching and conducting at Boston University. He lives in Boston with his wife, Debbie, and dog, Ruthie. JON NELSON is currently the songleader in residence at the Rashi Day School in Newton, MA. A graduate of the University of Massachusetts and Cambridge College, where he received his M.Ed., Jon plays bass guitar, acoustic guitar and sings lead. Jon and his wife Beth have three children, Evan, Ben Emily. He and his brother Josh compose the band's original songs.

DAN NICHOLS is one of the most popular and influential Jewish musicians in North America, performing over 200 concerts a year. His music has become an important part of the Reform Jewish movement, with synagogue youth and clergy alike incorporating it into their curriculum and services. His last two albums have garnered critical acclaim and a legion of growing fans. Songs like *L'takein (The Na Na Song)*, *B'tzelem Elohim*, *Kehilah Kedoshah*, and *My Heart is in the East* are some of the most popular songs in Reform Judaism today.

RICK RECHT is the top-touring musician in Jewish music, playing over 125 concerts a year in the United States and abroad. Recht is widely recognized for his appeal to youth and family audiences not only as an exceptional musician, singer/songwriter, and entertainer, but as a role model for involvement in Jewish life. He has become an icon for Jewish youth in the United States, elevating the medium of Jewish music as a powerful and effective tool for developing Jewish pride and identity among the masses. Recht has four top selling Jewish albums: *Tov*, *Shabbat Alive*, *Free to Be the Jew in Me*, and Rick's live CD and DVD, *The Hope*. His highly anticipated new album, *What Feels So Right*, has been receiving critical acclaim. Recht has earned several prestigious songwriting awards including the American Zionist Movement and the American Jewish Music Festival songwriting competitions. His pop and liturgical creations appear on dozens of national compilation albums and he has been commissioned to write theme songs for camps, Jewish special-interest groups, and synagogues where his original music appears in services and songbooks. He has been heard at NFTY, BBYO, URJ, USY, CAJE, Hillel Leaders Assembly, NAA, and other conferences. Born and raised in St. Louis, Missouri, Recht developed a strong Jewish identity attending Traditional Congregation, a conservative synagogue, and later, in high school, joined NFTY, where he was deeply influenced by Jewish music. After graduating from USC (Los Angeles, CA) and Music Institute (Hollywood, CA), Recht hit the road touring nationwide from LA to New York playing at clubs, colleges, and amphitheaters. After releasing 2 critically acclaimed secular albums, *Good Thing* and *Reality*, Recht returned to his Jewish roots with his debut Jewish album, *Tov*, in 1999. His shift to Jewish music marks the birth of a unique blend of pop, radio-friendly music with Hebrew, Jewish text, and social responsibility. Recht's songwriting combined with his trademark high-energy live show has drawn comparisons to acts such as Dave Matthews Band, Indigo Girls, Craig Taubman, and David Broza. He is the Artist in Residence at United Hebrew Congregation in St. Louis, Missouri and enjoys spending time with his wife, Elisa, three year old son, Kobi, and brand new boy Tal.

BETH SCHAFER is a much sought-after teacher and composer of contemporary Jewish music nationwide. She has been a featured performer at CAJE conferences and URJ National Biennials as well as on faculty for many camps and conferences including NAA, BBYO, and Kutz Camp. Beth is lauded most by fans and colleagues for her guitar playing: playing (and sometimes shredding) in many different styles on both acoustic and electric guitars. Beth attended the University of Miami School of Music on a jazz scholarship and has a degree in Theory and Composition. Her music can be found on many compilation CDs representing the best of Jewish music and tours with her band nationwide. Her song *Children of Freedom* which has become a signature American-Jewish anthem was also the theme song of a PBS special about building bridges between the Arab and Jewish communities. Her folk, rock, and alternative influences are very present in her unique and eclectic style. She has released 4 CDs and a songbook.

A world music ensemble creating and performing original music, **SHEVA** incorporates instruments from around the world and motives from the roots of Jewish and Arabic cultures as well as tribal cultures. Sheva was born in 1996 in a unique community situated in the Galilee Mountains, in northern Israel. Sheva's band members come from Muslim and Jewish backgrounds and the main theme in their songs is the call for peace in the Middle East and around the world. The combination of Biblical texts and innovative prayers for peace and kinship become an experience that joins together the four corners of the earth into one round planet. Since the summer of 2002, Sheva have been toured and performed around the world in: Australia, Europe, Canada, and America, to a rave reviews from audiences, press and national TV alike. Sheva is dedicated to the creation of an inspiring and uplifting musical experience, reminding every listening heart of the true peaceful and joyful nature of being.